Taste of
CHRISTMAS

Festive Family Fun
COOKBOOK

Recipes and Holiday Inspiration

© 2014 by Barbour Publishing, Inc.

Written and compiled by MariLee Parrish.

ISBN 978-1-62836-877-2

All scripture quotations are taken from the King James Version of the Bible.

Published by Barbour Books, an imprint of Barbour Publishing, Inc., P.O. Box 719, Uhrichsville, Ohio 44683, www.barbourbooks.com

Our mission is to publish and distribute inspirational products offering exceptional value and biblical encouragement to the masses.

ECPA Member of the
Evangelical Christian
Publishers Association

Printed in the United States of America.

Taste of
CHRISTMAS

Festive Family Fun
COOKBOOK

Recipes and Holiday Inspiration

BARBOUR BOOKS
An Imprint of Barbour Publishing, Inc.

Dashing through the snow
In a one-horse open sleigh,
O'er the fields we go
Laughing all the way.
Bells on bobtail ring,
Making spirits bright.
What fun it is to ride and sing
A sleighing song tonight!

Contents

This recipe book is meant to foster togetherness this Christmas season. Gather your family around the holiday calendar to plan fun family meals everyone can look forward to all month.

Big thanks go out to my friends Rhonda, Gail, Sara, and Leah (the owner of Peacock Pottery) for sharing special recipes from their own family festivities.

Many Christmas blessings!
MariLee Parrish

 Family Brunch

A new commandment I give unto you,
That ye love one another; as I have loved you,
that ye also love one another. By this shall all
men know that ye are my disciples,
if ye have love one to another.

JOHN 13:34–35

There's just nothing like a good family brunch. Omelets and blueberry pancakes, warm biscuits and fresh-squeezed orange juice. *MMMhhhmmm.* Add Christmas music and twinkling lights, and brunch is even more special! Make a point to plan several family brunches this holiday season. Each family member gets to add something to the menu, and everyone gets to help. And be sure to offer thanks to God, who is the Author of every good and perfect gift—including your family and a tasty brunch!

The Denver Omelet

2 teaspoons butter

2 tablespoons chopped fully cooked ham

1 tablespoon finely chopped bell pepper

1 tablespoon finely chopped onion

2 eggs, beaten

1 tablespoon milk

Salt and pepper to taste

¼ cup shredded Colby Jack cheese

Heat butter in skillet over medium-high heat. As butter melts, add ham, bell pepper, and onion. Cook for 2 to 3 minutes, stirring frequently. Meanwhile, in a separate bowl, beat eggs. Add milk and seasonings. Pour eggs into a separate skillet coated with nonstick spray (or melted butter). Slide pan back and forth over heat as they cook. Spread the eggs over bottom of pan with a fork as they thicken. Remove from heat when the eggs are fully cooked. Place the flat omelet on a plate and add the ham mixture. Top with half of cheese. Fold the omelet over and top with remaining cheese. Serve immediately.

Blueberry Buttermilk Pancakes

2 cups flour
¼ cup sugar
2 ¼ teaspoons baking powder
½ teaspoon baking soda
¼ teaspoon salt

2 eggs
2 cups buttermilk (or whole milk mixed with 1 teaspoon lemon juice)
¼ cup melted butter
1 cup blueberries

Sift together flour, sugar, baking powder, baking soda, and salt. In a separate bowl, beat eggs, buttermilk, and butter. Add to dry ingredients and stir lightly. Do not overmix. Batter should be lumpy. Heat some extra butter in a skillet over medium heat. Spoon ⅓ cup of batter into the skillet and add the desired amount of blueberries. Cook for 2 to 3 minutes on each side. Serve with whipped cream and syrup.

Breakfast Pizza

1 (8 count) package
  refrigerated crescent rolls

1 pound bulk sausage,
  cooked and drained

1 cup frozen hash browns, thawed

1 cup shredded sharp
  cheddar cheese

5 eggs

¼ cup milk

½ teaspoon salt

¼ teaspoon pepper

Press rolls in slightly greased 12-inch pizza pan. Seal perforations. Spoon sausage over crust. Sprinkle with potatoes. Top with cheddar cheese. In a bowl, beat together remaining ingredients. Pour into crust. Bake at 375 degrees for 25 to 30 minutes.

Grandma's Sausage Gravy & Biscuits

1 pound seasoned pork sausage
2 tablespoons grease
2 tablespoons flour

2 cups milk
Salt & pepper to taste
Prepared country biscuits

Brown sausage and drain all but 2 tablespoons grease. Stir in flour and gradually add milk. Stir over medium heat until gravy thickens. Add salt and pepper. Serve over split country biscuits.

Incredible Breakfast Casserole

12 to 16 ounces sausage
½ to 1 cup chopped onion
1 small can diced potatoes
8 large eggs

1½ cups milk
Salt and pepper to taste
5 slices bread, torn into 1-inch pieces
2 cups shredded cheddar cheese

Preheat oven to 350 degrees. Butter 2-quart baking dish. In large skillet, cook sausage with onion and potatoes. Whisk eggs with milk in bowl and season with salt and pepper; set aside. Arrange torn bread in bottom of baking dish. Sprinkle with sausage mixture and top with half the cheddar cheese. Pour egg mixture evenly over top and sprinkle with remaining cheese. Bake 35 to 40 minutes, until puffy and lightly browned.

Barn-Raising Biscuits

1 cup whole-wheat flour
2 cups all-purpose flour
2 tablespoons sugar
½ teaspoon salt
4½ teaspoons baking powder

¾ teaspoon cream of tartar
¾ cup butter or margarine
1 cup milk
1 egg

Preheat oven to 450 degrees. Combine flours, sugar, salt, baking powder, and cream of tartar in bowl. Cut in butter until mixture resembles thick cornmeal. Quickly stir in milk and egg. Turn out dough on floured cutting board and knead lightly. Roll or pat out to 1-inch thickness. Cut into 2-inch biscuits. Place on greased baking sheet. Bake for 12 to 15 minutes.

Blueberry Biscuits for Christmas Morning

BISCUITS:

2¼ cups flour, divided

½ cup sugar

1 tablespoon baking powder

½ teaspoon fresh grated lemon peel

¾ teaspoon salt

¼ teaspoon baking soda

⅓ cup shortening

1 egg, lightly beaten

¾ cup buttermilk

¾ cup frozen blueberries, do not thaw

TOPPING:

3 tablespoons butter, melted

2 tablespoons sugar

¼ teaspoon ground cinnamon

Dash ground nutmeg

In large bowl, mix 2 cups of flour with sugar, baking powder, lemon peel, salt, and baking soda. Cut in shortening until mixture has a large-grained, almost crumbly texture. Mix egg and buttermilk. Stir into flour mixture. Stir in frozen blueberries. Sprinkle remaining flour on countertop. Flour fingers and gently knead the dough a few times, just until dough begins to hold together. Pat dough into a 1/2-inch thick rectangle. Cut with floured 2-inch round cutter. Place biscuits 2 inches apart on a lightly greased baking sheet. Bake in center of a preheated 400 degree oven for 12 to 15 minutes, or until lightly browned. Combine topping ingredients and brush over the warm biscuits.

Breakfast Casserole

10 slices bacon, diced
6 slices bread, lightly buttered
6 eggs, slightly beaten
2 cups milk

1 teaspoon salt
¼ teaspoon dry mustard
¼ teaspoon ground paprika

Cook bacon until browned and drain on paper towels. Cut bread into small pieces. In lightly buttered 2-quart casserole, layer bread pieces and bacon. In a bowl, whisk together eggs, milk, salt, mustard, and paprika. Pour over bread and bacon. Bake at 350 degrees for 45 minutes until puffy and a knife inserted in center comes out clean.

Blue Ridge Cinnamon Rolls

Rolls:
½ cup warm water
2 packages dry yeast
2 tablespoon sugar
1 package vanilla pudding mix
½ cup butter, melted
2 eggs

1 teaspoon salt
6 cups flour

Filling:
1 cup butter, softened
1 cup light brown sugar
4 teaspoons cinnamon

Mix water, yeast, and sugar together until dissolved. Set aside. In large bowl prepare pudding mix according to package directions. Add butter, eggs, and salt. Mix to blend well. Add yeast mixture and blend well. Gradually add flour. Transfer to lightly floured surface and knead dough until smooth. Place in greased bowl; cover and let rise in a warm area until doubled in size. Punch down dough and let rise again until doubled. Roll out dough on a floured surface. Take 1 cup soft butter and spread over surface. In bowl mix 2 cups brown sugar and 4 teaspoons cinnamon; sprinkle over the top. Roll up tightly. Cut with a sharp knife. Place cinnamon rolls on lightly greased cookie sheet 2 inches apart; lightly press each roll down. Cover and let rise to double again. Bake at 350 degrees for 15 to 20 minutes. Remove when they start to turn golden. Do not over bake. Frost warm rolls with a cream cheese frosting. Makes about 20 large cinnamon rolls.

Buttermilk Biscuits

¼ cup shortening
2 cups self-rising flour, sifted

¼ teaspoon baking soda
1 cup buttermilk, minus 1 tablespoon

Cut or rub shortening into flour and baking soda until the mixture resembles coarse crumbs. Add buttermilk and stir with fork. Turn dough onto lightly floured board and knead until smooth. Roll dough out about ½-inch thick and cut with floured round cutter. Place on lightly greased baking sheet and refrigerate till morning. Before serving, bake in preheated 450 degree oven for 10 to 12 minutes.

Make-Ahead Mexican Egg Casserole

1 small sweet onion, chopped
¼ cup green pepper, chopped
3 tablespoons butter
1½ cups corn

¼ cup black olives, sliced
8 eggs, beaten
1 cup sausage, cooked
1 cup sharp cheddar cheese, shredded

In a large skillet, sauté onion and green pepper in butter, until tender. Stir in corn, olives, and eggs. Add sausage and cheese, and cook until eggs are done. Pour into greased 9x13-inch pan and cool. Freeze for 1 hour. Wrap in double layers of foil, label, and store in freezer for up to 1 month. To serve: thaw completely in refrigerator; then heat in 300 degree oven for about 20 minutes. Serve with salsa.

Grammy's Baked Sausage Casserole

12 slices white bread, cubed
1 pound sausage, cooked and
drained
1 cup shredded cheddar cheese

6 eggs
2 cups milk
1 teaspoon salt
½ teaspoon pepper

Evenly sprinkle the bread in greased 9x13-inch pan. Spoon meat over bread and top with cheese. In separate bowl, beat eggs, milk, salt, and pepper. Pour over bread mixture. Bake at 350 degrees for 20 minutes or until done.

Avocado and Cheese Scramble

¼ cup green pepper, diced
¼ cup onion, diced
2 tablespoons butter
8 large eggs
¼ cup milk

2 tablespoons fresh cilantro, chopped
Salt and pepper to taste
1 cup shredded sharp cheddar cheese
1 avocado, peeled and sliced

Sauté pepper and onion in butter. Beat eggs and milk until well combined. Add cilantro and season with salt and pepper. Place in buttered skillet and scramble. Cook for 3 to 5 more minutes. Top with cheese and avocado. Serve with salsa and sour cream, if desired.

Sausage Muffins

4 cups biscuit baking mix
2 cups cornmeal
6 eggs
Dash pepper

3½ cups milk
2 pounds breakfast sausage, cooked and crumbled
3 cups shredded cheddar cheese

Mix together biscuit mix, cornmeal, eggs, pepper, and milk. Add sausage and cheese and mix well. Spoon into paper liners and place in muffin pan. Bake at 375 degrees for 12 minutes or until set.

Sausage Casserole

12 slices bread

3 tablespoons butter

2 pounds bulk sausage, browned and drained

2 cups sharp cheddar cheese, shredded

8 eggs

1 quart half-and-half

1 teaspoons salt

Dash pepper

1 teaspoon dry mustard

Remove crusts from bread. Butter 9x13-inch baking pan. Then spread remaining butter evenly on 6 slices of bread and layer in pan with the buttered side facing down. Top with sausage and then with cheese. Cover with remaining bread buttered with the buttered side facing up. Combine remaining ingredients in a bowl and mix well. Pour over top of bread and cover. Refrigerate overnight. The next morning, bake at 350 degrees for 1 hour. Serve or freeze for up to 2 months. If frozen, thaw completely before warming slowly in a 300 degree oven.

Pumpkin Chocolate Chip Muffins

1½ cups sugar

1½ cups light brown sugar

¾ cup plus 3 tablespoons canola oil

1 (15 ounce) can pumpkin puree

4 large eggs

3⅓ cups flour

2½ teaspoons baking soda

2 teaspoons salt

2 tablespoons cinnamon

1 teaspoon nutmeg

¼ teaspoon cloves

1 cup mini chocolate chips

In a mixing bowl, beat sugars with oil, pumpkin puree, and eggs until well blended.

Combine flour, baking soda, salt, and spices in a bowl; stir into pumpkin mixture until well blended. Stir in chocolate chips. Fill greased muffin cups ¾ full. Bake at 350 degrees for 25 minutes, or until firm. Freeze in sealed sandwich bags and then place in heavy-duty freezer bags. Allow to thaw before serving.

French Toast Sticks

4 eggs lightly beaten
2 teaspoons cinnamon
2 teaspoons sugar

⅓ cup milk
8 to 10 thick slices white bread

Whisk together eggs, cinnamon, sugar, and milk in a shallow dish. Dip both sides of bread into the egg mixture and cook in a greased frying pan until each side is browned. Cut each slice into three rectangles. Allow to cool and place on cookie sheet, flash freeze for about 30 minutes. Then place in freezer bag and freeze for up to 3 months. To serve: warm in microwave for 1 to 2 minutes and dip in warm syrup.

To make your brunch more festive, place a special ornament or Christmas decoration at each table setting. Serve a special Christmas punch along with coffee and juice.

Holiday Brunch Pineapple Punch

1 quart water
2 cups sugar
2 cups pineapple juice

Juice of 6 lemons
3 pints chilled ginger ale

Boil water and sugar for twenty minutes; then add the pineapple and lemon juice. Stir and cool completely. The ginger ale should be added just before serving. As an added touch, freeze red and green maraschino cherries with water in ice cube trays.

Bacon and Cheese Breakfast Pizza

1 (9-inch) refrigerated pie crust
½ pound bacon, cooked and
   crumbled
1 cup shredded cheddar cheese

4 eggs
12 ounces sour cream
1 teaspoon parsley

Roll pastry to fit a 12-inch pizza pan. Bake at 425 degrees for 5 minutes. Sprinkle bacon and cheese evenly over crust. Beat eggs, sour cream, and parsley until smooth. Pour over pizza. Bake for 20 to 25 minutes or until pizza is puffy and golden brown.

Sausage Scramble

6 eggs

4 sausage links, precooked and sliced

½ cup cheddar cheese

Salt and pepper to taste

Beat eggs until well combined. Place in buttered skillet and scramble. Add sausage, cheese, salt, and pepper. Cook for 3 to 5 more minutes until sausage is heated through.

Easy Brunch Casserole

2 cups stuffing mix in the canister
2 cups milk
½ pound maple sausage, cooked and crumbled

6 eggs
1 cup shredded cheddar cheese
½ teaspoon salt
¼ teaspoon pepper

Mix all ingredients in large bowl. Spoon into greased 9x13-inch baking pan. Bake at 350 degrees for 45 minutes or until knife inserted in center comes out clean.

French Toast Casserole

1 (16-ounce) loaf cinnamon raisin bread, cubed
6 large eggs, beaten

3 cups milk
2 teaspoons vanilla extract
Powdered sugar

Layer the bread cubes evenly in a greased 9x13-inch baking dish. Beat eggs, milk, and vanilla in separate bowl. Pour mixture over bread cubes. Cover and refrigerate for at least 2 hours or overnight. Bake for 50 minutes at 350 degrees or until golden brown. Sprinkle with powdered sugar. Serve warm topped with syrup.

Cheesy Hash Brown Casserole

1 (32 ounce) bag frozen shredded hash browns

2 (10 ounce) cans of cream of potato soup

16 ounces sour cream

2 cups shredded sharp cheddar cheese

1 cup Parmesan cheese

¼ cup real bacon bits

Combine all ingredients, and stir well. Spoon into greased 9x13-inch baking dish. Bake at 350 degrees for 40 minutes or until golden brown.

Spinach Soufflé

1 large egg

⅓ cup milk

⅓ cup grated parmesan cheese

1 teaspoon garlic salt

⅛ teaspoon pepper

2 (10 ounce) packages frozen spinach, thawed

Whisk together all ingredients except spinach in a large bowl. Fold in spinach. Bake at 350 degrees in lightly buttered casserole dish for 20 minutes, or until set. Serve with sliced tomato for a red and green festive dish!

Potato Skins

8 large potatoes, baked and cooled

2 tablespoons butter, melted

1 cup real bacon pieces

1 small sweet onion, diced

½ cup shredded cheddar cheese

Cut potatoes in half and scoop out the middles (save for another meal). Brush insides with butter, and fill with bacon and onions. Top with cheese. Bake for 15 minutes at 450 degrees.

Breakfast Lasagna

½ cup sour cream
1 (10 ounce) can cream of
   mushroom soup
1 (32 ounce) bag frozen hash
   browns

1 sweet onion, diced
1 pound cooked bacon, diced
1 cup shredded cheddar cheese
1 cup shredded mozzarella cheese

Mix sour cream and mushroom soup until well blended. In lasagna pan, layer hash browns, soup mixture, onions, bacon, and cheese in that order. Cover and bake at 325 degrees for 1 hour. Remove foil and bake 5 more minutes.

Breakfast Skillet

½ pound bulk pork sausage

2 cups frozen shredded hash browns

1 (10 ounce) can diced tomatoes and green chilies, drained

8 ounces of pasteurized prepared cheese, cut up

6 eggs

2 tablespoons water

Brown and drain sausage. Leave in skillet. Add hash browns and tomatoes to skillet. Cook for 5 minutes and add cheese product. In separate bowl, whisk eggs and water together. Pour evenly over ingredients in skillet. Place skillet in oven. Bake for 20 minutes at 375 degrees or until egg mixture is set. Let stand 5 minutes before serving.

Bacon and Potato Casserole

4 cups frozen shredded hash brown potatoes

½ cup finely chopped onion

8 ounces bacon, cooked and crumbled

1 cup shredded cheddar cheese

1 (12 ounce) can evaporated milk

1 large egg, lightly beaten

1 teaspoon seasoned salt

¼ teaspoon pepper

Layer ½ potatoes, ½ onion, ½ bacon, and ½ cheese in greased 8-inch baking dish; repeat layers. Combine evaporated milk, egg, and seasoned salt in small bowl. Pour evenly over potato mixture. Cover and bake for 55 to 60 minutes at 350 degrees. Uncover and bake for 5 more minutes. Let stand for 10 minutes before serving.

Take time this Christmastide
to go a little way apart,
And with the help of God prepare
the house that is in your heart.

ANONYMOUS

Throw It in a Pot

O come, let us worship and bow down:
*let us kneel before the L*ORD *our maker.*

PSALM 95:6

Cherry Cobbler

2 (21 ounce) cans cherry
pie filling

1 (18 ounce) package yellow cake
mix

¼ cup butter, softened

Pour pie filling into slow cooker and spread evenly. In separate bowl, combine dry cake mix with butter until it is crumbly. Sprinkle cake mix over pie filling. Cook on low for 3 to 4 hours. Serve warm with vanilla ice cream, and sprinkle with chopped pecans.

Easy Chicken Chili

1 pound boneless, skinless chicken breast, cut into bite-size pieces

1 (1 ounce) package taco seasoning mix

3 (14 ounce) cans diced tomatoes with chilies and garlic, undrained

2 (15 ounce) cans white beans, drained and rinsed

Combine all ingredients in slow cooker. Cook on low for 7 to 9 hours or until chicken is tender and no longer pink.

Christmas Rice Pudding

1½ cups cooked rice
1 (16 ounce) container of half-and-half
¾ cup raisins

3 eggs
⅔ cup sugar
2 teaspoons vanilla
½ teaspoon nutmeg

Lightly butter slow cooker. Whisk together half-and-half, eggs, sugar, and vanilla. Beat well. Pour into slow cooker. Stir in rice and raisins. Sprinkle nutmeg on top. Cook on high for 30 minutes. Stir well. Cook on low for 2 to 3 more hours.

Make-Ahead Party Meatballs

2 pounds lean ground beef
1 small sweet onion, grated
2 teaspoons garlic salt
⅛ teaspoon pepper
½ cup corn flakes, crushed

2 eggs, beaten
1½ cups chili sauce
Juice of 1 lemon
½ cup grape jelly

Thoroughly mix ground beef, onion, garlic salt, pepper, corn flakes, and eggs. Shape into 2-inch balls and place in lightly greased baking pan. Combine remaining ingredients in a saucepan and simmer 5 minutes. Pour over meatballs. Bake at 350 degrees for 30 minutes. Allow to cool. Skim off fat and store in freezer containers. Freeze for up to 3 months. To serve: reheat in slow cooker or microwave.

Queso Dip

2 (15 ounce) cans tomatoes with chilies

2 pounds processed cheese, chopped

Pour into a slow cooker and mix. Cook on high setting for 20 to 25 minutes. Serve with tortilla chips. If desired, add cooked and crumbled sausage to make this more filling.

Tahnee's Tuna Casserole

2 (5 ounce) cans tuna, drained

1 (10 ounce) can cream of celery soup

3 hard boiled eggs, chopped

½ cup diced celery

½ cup mayonnaise

¼ teaspoon pepper

1 cup crushed potato chips

Spray slow cooker with non-stick spray. Place all ingredients in slow cooker and mix well. Cook on low for 6 hours.

Comfort in a Pot

¾ cup brown sugar
4 cups water
¼ teaspoon salt
¼ teaspoon nutmeg
¼ teaspoon cinnamon

¼ teaspoon allspice
⅛ teaspoon ground cloves
2 (16 ounce) cans jellied cranberry sauce
2 cups pineapple juice
1 tablespoon butter

Mix all ingredients together in slow cooker except butter. Stir well. Cook on low for 3 to 4 hours. Add butter just before serving.

Glory to God in the highest,
and on earth peace,
good will toward men.

LUKE 2:14

Slow Cooker Fruit Punch

8 cups water

1 (12 ounce) can frozen cranberry-raspberry juice concentrate, thawed

1 (12 ounce) can frozen lemonade concentrate, thawed

¼ cup sugar

¼ teaspoon cinnamon

Combine all ingredients in slow cooker and cook on low for 4 hours or until heated through.

Coconut Sweet Potatoes

2 pounds sweet potatoes, peeled and shredded

1/3 cup brown sugar

1/4 cup butter, melted

1/4 cup coconut

1/2 cup pecans, chopped and toasted

1/4 teaspoon ground cinnamon

1/4 teaspoon coconut flavoring

1/4 teaspoon vanilla

Place sweet potatoes in slow cooker. Combine sugar, butter, coconut, pecans, and cinnamon in a bowl. Drizzle over sweet potatoes. Cook on low for 6 to 8 hours. Add coconut flavoring and vanilla in the last hour of cooking.

Holiday Green Bean Casserole

1 (28 ounce) package frozen cut green beans

1 onion, chopped

1 cup roasted red bell pepper strips, chopped

½ teaspoon salt

¼ teaspoon pepper

1 (10 ounce) jar Alfredo sauce

1 (2.5 ounce) can french fried onions

In slow cooker, combine all ingredients except half of fried onions. Cook on high for 3 to 4 hours, stirring after 1 hour. Top with remaining fried onions and serve.

Slow Cooker Cheesy Potatoes

1 (10 ounce) can condensed cream
of mushroom soup

1 (8 ounce) container sour cream

1½ cups shredded sharp cheddar
cheese

1 (32 ounce) package frozen hash
brown potatoes

Spray slow cooker with cooking spray. Combine soup, sour cream, and cheese in medium bowl and mix well. Pour half of potatoes into prepared slow cooker. Top with half of sour cream mixture. Add remaining potatoes and top with sour cream mixture, spreading evenly over all. Cook on high for 4 hours.

Slow Cooker Mac and Cheese

1 (16 ounce) package macaroni, cooked and drained

½ pound processed cheese

1 (10 ounce) can cheese soup

1 cup butter

1 teaspoon salt

2 cups milk

Combine all ingredients in slow cooker. Cook on low for 1 hour, stir.

Broccoli Rice Casserole

1 (10 ounce) can condensed cream of mushroom soup

1 (8 ounce) jar processed cheese sauce

1 cup milk

1 cup minute rice

1 small onion, chopped

1 teaspoon garlic salt

1 (16 ounce) package frozen broccoli cuts, thawed and drained

In slow cooker, combine soup, cheese sauce, milk, rice, onion, and garlic salt. Add broccoli and mix well. Cover and cook on low for 4 to 5 hours.

Uncle Cory's White Chili

- 1 pound boneless, skinless chicken breast, cooked and cut into bite-size pieces
- 1 medium onion, chopped
- 1½ teaspoons garlic powder
- 2 (16 ounce) cans great northern white beans, drained
- 1 (15 ounce) can chicken broth
- 1 teaspoon salt
- 1 teaspoon oregano
- ½ teaspoon pepper
- ¼ teaspoon red pepper
- 2 cans (4 ounce) diced green chilies
- 1 cup light sour cream
- ½ cup half-and-half

Add all ingredients to slow cooker except sour cream and half-and-half. Cook on high for 3 to 4 hours. Add sour cream and half-and-half in the last hour of cooking. Serve immediately.

Easy Country-Style BBQ Ribs

8 boneless beef ribs

2 (18 ounce) bottles mesquite-flavored barbecue sauce

Place ribs in single layer in slow cooker; cover completely with barbecue sauce. Cook on medium heat for 8 to 10 hours.

Apple Pecan Dump Cake

1 (21 ounce) can apple pie filling
1 package yellow cake mix

½ cup butter
½ cup chopped pecans (or your favorite nuts)

Put pie filling into slow cooker. Separately, cut butter into cake mix, and then sprinkle over pie filling. Sprinkle pecans over top. Cook on low for 2 to 3 hours. Serve warm with ice cream.

Honey Apple Tea

1 (12 ounce) can frozen apple juice concentrate

2 tablespoons instant tea

1 tablespoon honey

1 cinnamon stick

Prepare apple juice according to directions on label. Pour into slow cooker with remaining ingredients. Heat on low for 2 hours. Serve warm.

Southwest Chicken Stew

3 boneless, skinless chicken breasts

1 (15 ounce) can diced tomatoes with green chilies

1 (15 ounce) can black beans, undrained

2 (10½ ounce) cans cream of chicken soup

3 cups corn

2 cups of chicken broth

Put all ingredients in slow cooker. Cook on low for 8 hours. Remove chicken and shred or cut into chunks. Return to slow cooker and serve.

What I'd like to have for Christmas
I can tell you in a minute—
The family all around me
And the home with laughter in it.

EDGAR A. GUEST

Triple Chocolate Delight

1 (18 ounce) package chocolate fudge cake mix

1 pint sour cream

1 (4 ounce) package instant chocolate pudding

1 (12 ounce) bag milk chocolate chips

¾ cup oil

4 eggs

1 cup water

Spray slow cooker with non-stick spray. Mix all ingredients. Pour into slow cooker. Cook on low for 4 to 5 hours. Serve warm with ice cream.

Easy Cherry Chocolate Dessert

1 (21 ounce) can cherry pie filling

1 (18 ounce) package chocolate
   fudge cake mix

½ cup butter

Place pie filling in slow cooker. Combine dry cake mix and butter.
Sprinkle over filling. Cover and cook on low for 3 hours.

Winter Potato Chowder

1 (5 ounce) package scalloped
  potato mix (including sauce
  mix)
4 cups chicken broth
2 onions, chopped

2 cups half-and-half
⅓ cup flour
⅛ teaspoon white pepper
1 teaspoon dried marjoram leaves

Add potato mix, broth, and onions to slow cooker. Stir well to blend. Cook on low for 7 hours. In separate bowl mix together half-and-half and flour with a wire whisk until smooth. Slowly stir this mixture into the slow cooker. Stir until well blended, then add pepper and marjoram. Cook on low for 1 more hour, stirring occasionally. Add baked diced ham in the last hour of cooking, if desired.

Slow Cooker Winter Pot Roast

1 onion, chopped
¼ cup water
4 dried shiitake mushrooms, rinsed, stemmed, and crumbled
¼ cup ketchup
¼ cup red cooking wine
2 tablespoons Dijon mustard
2 tablespoons Worcestershire sauce
½ teaspoon salt
⅛ teaspoon pepper
1 teaspoon garlic powder
3 pounds chuck roast, trimmed
2 tablespoons cornstarch
3 tablespoons water

Add all ingredients to slow cooker except meat, cornstarch, and water. Mix well. Add meat. Cook on low for 8 hours. Remove meat, but keep warm. Dissolve cornstarch in water and stir into slow cooker. Cook on high for 15 more minutes. Serve sauce with sliced meat.

Quick & Festive Salsa Chicken

4 boneless chicken breasts   3 (16 ounce) jars tomato salsa
1 (28 ounce) can enchilada sauce

Add all ingredients to slow cooker. Cook on high for 5 to 6 hours. Shred chicken and serve with rice and tortillas.

Pulled Pork Burritos

2-pound boneless pork loin roast
1 medium sweet onion,
   thinly sliced
2 cups barbecue sauce

¼ cup chunky salsa
2 tablespoons chili powder
3 teaspoons taco seasoning

Place pork roast in slow cooker and arrange onion on top. In separate bowl, combine remaining ingredients and mix well. Pour over pork. Cook on low setting for 8 to 10 hours. Shred pork and spoon mixture into tortillas along with shredded lettuce, chopped tomatoes, shredded cheese, and sour cream.

Spinach Bow-Tie Pasta

1½ pounds lean ground beef, browned with 1 medium onion (chopped) and 1 clove minced garlic

1 (16 ounce) jar tomato sauce

1 (14 ounce) can stewed tomatoes

1 teaspoon oregano

1 teaspoon Italian seasoning

Salt and pepper, to taste

1 (10 ounce) package frozen chopped spinach, thawed

1 (16 ounce) package bow-tie pasta, cooked and drained

½ cup grated Parmesan cheese

1½ cups shredded mozzarella cheese

Add all ingredients to slow cooker except spinach, pasta, and cheese. Cook on high for 4 hours. Stir in the cooked pasta, spinach, and cheese during the last ½ hour of cooking. Continue cooking until pasta is tender.

Slow Cooker Meatballs

1 (2 ounce) package dry onion soup mix

3 cloves garlic, minced

1 (10 ounce) jar beef gravy

3 tablespoons water

⅛ teaspoon pepper

3 pounds frozen cooked meatballs

Combine all ingredients except meatballs in slow cooker and mix well. Add meatballs and stir carefully. Cook on low for 4 to 5 hours. Serve with noodles or rice.

Slow Cooker Tips

Remove cooked food from the slow cooker before refrigeration. If left in the slow cooker for storage, the food won't cool down quickly enough to prevent the growth of bacteria. The liner is made of very thick material and does not cool quickly.

Each time you lift the lid to check your slow cooker, heat escapes. Each time you lift the lid while using the "low" setting, you should extend the cook time by a half an hour.

Using the "high" setting can cause overcooking. The high setting is best used to bring meat up to a safe temperature quickly before beginning slow cooking.

Do not fill a slow cooker more than two-thirds full. The foods will not cook properly if the cooker is overfilled.

Swiss Steak in a Pot

2 (2 ounce) packages onion soup mix

2 (10 ounce) cans cream of mushroom soup

1 soup can full of water

3 pounds round steak, trimmed and cut into serving sizes

Mix dry onion soup mix, mushroom soup, and water in slow cooker. Add steak and spoon mixture on top of steak. Cook on low for 8 hours. Serve with mashed potatoes or rice.

Peachy Pork Chops

Salt and pepper
6 pork chops
1 (29 ounce) can peach halves,
  reserving the syrup

¼ cup brown sugar
¼ teaspoon ground cloves
1 (8 ounce) can tomato sauce
¼ cup vinegar

Salt and pepper each pork chop and brown lightly on both sides in a skillet. Drain and place in slow cooker. Top with drained peaches. In separate bowl, combine brown sugar, cloves, tomato sauce, vinegar, and ¼ cup syrup from peaches. Pour tomato mixture over all. Cook on low for 6 to 8 hours or until chops are tender. Serve with mashed potatoes or rice.

Rigatoni Pizza in a Pot

1½ pounds hamburger, browned and drained

8 ounces rigatoni, cooked

1 pound pepperoni

1 cup sliced mushrooms

2 cups mozzarella cheese, shredded

1 onion, diced

1 (10 ounce) can mushroom soup

1 (16 ounce) can spaghetti sauce

Layer in slow cooker and cook on high for 2 to 3 hours.

Slow Cooker Beef Stroganoff

1 tablespoon olive oil

1 cup water

2 (6 ounce) cans sliced
mushrooms

1 (2 ounce) package onion soup
mix

2 pounds stew beef, cut into bite-
sized pieces

1 tablespoon flour

1 cup sour cream

Stir together oil, water, mushrooms, and soup mix. Add to slow cooker.
Add beef and mix. Cook on high for 5 to 6 hours. In separate bowl,
combine flour and sour cream. Add to slow cooker and cook ½ hour
longer. Serve over hot cooked noodles.

Simple Slow Cooker Ratatouille

This is a great meal to serve on movie night!
Rent Disney's version of *Ratatouille* and
enjoy a fun family night at home.

1 medium eggplant, sliced thin

2 pounds fresh tomatoes,
  sliced thin

2 medium zucchini, sliced thin

2 green bell peppers, sliced thin

½ cup olive oil

1 garlic clove, chopped

1 teaspoon salt

½ teaspoon pepper

Lightly brown all vegetables in olive oil with the garlic clove. Place
vegetables and oil from the skillet in slow cooker and season with salt
and pepper. Cover and cook on high 2 to 3 hours or until vegetables
are tender.

And so it was, that, while they were there, the days were accomplished that she should be delivered. And she brought forth her firstborn son, and wrapped him in swaddling clothes, and laid him in a manger; because there was no room for them in the inn.

Luke 2:6-7

Quick & Easy Meals

For unto you is born this day in the city of David a Saviour, which is Christ the Lord.

LUKE 2:11

Beef Tips with Noodles

2 pounds lean stew meat,
cut into bite-sized pieces
1 (10 ounce) can cream of
mushroom soup

1 package dry onion soup mix
1 cup lemon-lime soda
Cooked noodles or rice

Place meat in 2-quart casserole dish. Top with soup and onion soup mix. Add soda. Do not stir. Cover and bake at 275 degrees for 4 hours. Do not open oven door during cooking. Let stand for 30 minutes before serving. Serve over cooked noodles or rice.

Festive Chili and Cheese

1 pound ground beef, browned
   with 1 chopped onion
2 tablespoons chili seasoning
1 (10 ounce) can tomato soup
½ cup water
2 eggs, slightly beaten

1 cup milk
2 cup corn chips, crushed
1 cup shredded Monterey Jack
   cheese
1 cup sour cream
½ cup shredded sharp cheddar

Add beef, onion, seasoning, soup, and water to a large skillet. Simmer 5 minutes. Add eggs and milk. Cook and stir until bubbly. Add corn chips and Monterey Jack cheese. Pour into a casserole dish. Bake at 350 degrees for 35 minutes. Top with sour cream and cheddar cheese during last 5 minutes of cooking.

Super-Quick Meat Loaf

1 pound ground beef
1 package dry onion soup mix

1 jar plain spaghetti sauce

Mix ground beef and onion soup mix; divide and shape into 2 loaves.
Place loaves in deep baking dish. Pour spaghetti sauce over loaves.
Bake at 350 degrees for 1 hour.

Peacock Pottery Swiss Vegetable Casserole

1 (16 ounce) package California mix vegetables, cooked

2 tablespoons milk

1 (10 ounce) can cream of mushroom soup

½ cup sour cream

1 cup shredded Swiss cheese, divided

1 (2.8 ounce) can French fried onions, divided

½ teaspoon salt

½ teaspoon pepper

Preheat oven to 350 degrees. Put cooked vegetables in a bowl with milk, soup, sour cream, ½ cup cheese, and ½ can of French fried onions. Mix, then add salt and pepper; mix again. Pour into casserole dish and bake covered for 50 minutes. Remove from oven, then top with remaining cheese and onions; return to oven, uncovered, for another 10 minutes or until browned.

Family Barbecue Burgers

4 to 6 hamburger patties
1 cup ketchup
2 tablespoons mustard

½ cup sugar
1 tablespoon vinegar

Grill hamburger patties until done. Combine ketchup, mustard, sugar, and vinegar. Place spoonfuls of mixture in bottom of shallow baking dish; place grilled hamburgers on top. Pour remaining sauce over burgers. Cover and bake at 325 degrees for 1 hour. Serve on buns with chips and pickles.

Microwave Chicken Lasagna

¼ cup cilantro, chopped

½ cup onion, chopped

2 cups shredded cheddar cheese, divided

1 (28 ounce) can enchilada sauce

12 tortillas

8 ounces cream cheese, softened

3 cups cooked chicken, shredded

Mix cilantro, onion, and 1 cup cheddar cheese. Spread ⅔ cup enchilada sauce in microwavable dish. Pour remaining sauce into large bowl. Dip 4 tortillas into sauce and arrange in baking pan. Spread ⅓ of the cream cheese over tortillas. Top with 1 cup chicken. Repeat layers twice. Top with remaining sauce and cheddar cheese. Cover and microwave on high for 13 minutes or until heated through.

Born thy people to deliver,
Born a child and yet a King,
Born to reign in us forever,
Now thy gracious kingdom bring.

CHARLES WESLEY

Fiesta Fajitas

2 to 3 boneless, skinless chicken breasts, cut into strips

2 tablespoons oil

1 green and 1 red bell pepper, cut into strips

1 small sweet onion, sliced

Flour tortillas

Sauté chicken in oil in large skillet for 4 minutes. Add peppers and onion; cook over low heat for 5 minutes or until tender. Put mixture into tortillas. Top with salsa, cheese, and sour cream, if desired.

Cheeseburger and Fries Casserole

1 pound frozen french fries, baked according to package directions

1 pound ground beef, browned

1 (14 ounce) can sloppy joe mix

2 cups cheddar cheese, shredded

Place prepared fries in the bottom of 9x13-inch casserole dish. Spoon browned hamburger on top of fries. Add sloppy joe mix. Top with cheese. Bake in oven at 350 degrees for 30 minutes or until heated through.

Easy Cheesy Casserole

1 pound ground beef

1 box shells and cheese dinner mix

1 (10 ounce) can condensed cream
  of mushroom soup

1½ to 2 cups shredded cheddar
  cheese

Brown ground beef; drain. Prepare shells and cheese according to
package directions. Combine beef, shells and cheese, and soup in
2-quart casserole dish. Top with cheese. Bake at 350 degrees for 25 to
30 minutes or until heated through.

Italian Sausage Sandwiches

2 tablespoons butter
1 small sweet onion, sliced
1 green bell pepper, sliced
1 red bell pepper, sliced

6 to 8 precooked sausage links
Hot dog buns
Provolone cheese

Sauté onion and peppers in butter. Add sausage links and heat until warmed through. Place 2 sausage links in a hot dog bun. Add as many onions and peppers as you like. Top with 1 piece of provolone cheese. Place on a cookie sheet and broil on low until cheese is melted.

Italian Meatball Soup

1 pound frozen fully cooked
  meatballs
1 (16 ounce) jar spaghetti sauce
1 teaspoon oregano

2½ cups water
1 (20 ounce) package frozen
  cheese tortellini
½ cup grated Parmesan cheese

In large pot, combine meatballs, sauce, oregano, and water. Bring to a boil. Reduce heat, stir in tortellini, and simmer for 10 minutes or until meatballs and pasta are tender. Sprinkle with Parmesan cheese. Serve with a Caesar salad.

Chicken Pasta Salad

6 ounces multi-color pasta noodles, cooked, drained, and rinsed

1 celery stick, chopped

1 carrot, chopped

1 green onion, chopped

6 to 8 cherry tomatoes, cut in half

¼ cup sliced black olives

2 baked chicken breasts, chopped

¼ cup Parmesan cheese

½ cup Italian dressing

Mix all ingredients together and serve.

Creamy Italian Chicken

4 small boneless, skinless chicken breasts, coated lightly with flour

1 tablespoon olive oil

¾ cup chicken broth

4 ounces cream cheese, cubed

2 tablespoons Italian dressing

In a large skillet, add chicken to oil and cook for 5 to 6 minutes on each side until done. Remove chicken and reserve drippings. Add broth to drippings and stir. Add cream cheese and Italian dressing. Cook for 3 minutes until cream cheese is melted, stirring constantly with whisk. Return chicken to skillet and coat with sauce. Cook 2 more minutes. Serve with hot buttered noodles or rice.

Rhonda's Cheese and Chicken Dinner

2 (5 ounce) cans chunky chicken

2 teaspoons garlic

½ (15 ounce) can tomatoes with chilies

¼ cup onion

1 pound processed cheese, cubed

1 package corn tortillas

1 (10 ounce) can cream of chicken soup

Mix chicken, garlic, tomatoes, and onion with cubed cheese. In 2-quart greased pan, tear ⅓ of corn tortillas in strips and put ⅓ chicken mix next. Layer. Pour soup on top. Cook at 350 for 20 minutes.

Beef and Broccoli

1 tablespoon butter
¾ pound thin beef strips
1 small sweet onion, sliced
2 cups fresh broccoli florets

½ cup fresh mushrooms, sliced
1 (2 ounce) package brown gravy mix
1 cup water
¼ teaspoon pepper

In a large skillet, heat butter over medium-high heat. Add beef strips and onion and sauté for 3 to 4 minutes; add broccoli and mushrooms. In a separate bowl, combine gravy mix, water, and pepper. Pour over beef mixture. Stir and bring to a boil. Cover and simmer 5 to 8 minutes or until broccoli is tender.

No-Peek Steak

4 pounds round steak, cut into squares

1 (10 ounce) can condensed cream of mushroom soup

1 (10 ounce) can condensed cream of celery soup

1 (10 ounce) can condensed cream of onion soup

1 can sliced mushroom

Place steak in casserole dish. Combine soups and pour over steak. Top with mushrooms. Bake at 225 degrees for 4 hours. Don't peek!

Porcupine Meatballs

2 pounds ground beef
2 (11 ounce) cans tomato soup
2½ teaspoon chili powder, divided
Salt and pepper to taste

1 egg
1 medium onion, finely chopped
¼ cup rice (not instant)

In skillet, brown ground beef and set aside. Heat soup to boil and then reduce to simmer. With each can of soup, add 2 cans water. Add to soup: 1 teaspoon chili powder and salt and pepper to taste. Let soup mixture simmer while mixing the following ingredients in large bowl: egg, onion, rice, remaining chili powder, and ground beef. Salt and pepper to taste. Mix well and shape into meatballs. Be careful not to pack meatballs too tightly. Drop meatballs into hot soup mixture and bring to boil. Reduce heat and simmer 1½ hours.

Speedy Beefy Stroganoff

1½ pounds ground beef

1 medium onion, chopped

2 (10 ounce) cans condensed
   cheddar cheese soup

1 can sliced mushrooms with juice

Salt and pepper to taste

In large skillet, brown ground beef and onion; drain. Stir in soup and mushrooms with juice. Season to taste. Simmer until heated through. Serve over noodles, rice, or toast.

Beef Taco Bake

1 small sweet onion, chopped
1 (10 ounce) can tomato soup
1 cup salsa
½ cup water

8 corn tortillas cut into 1-inch pieces
1 pound ground beef, browned and drained
1 cup shredded cheddar cheese

Add onion, soup, salsa, water, and tortillas to the beef. Add half of the cheese and mix well. Spoon into baking dish and cover. Bake at 400 degrees for 30 minutes. Sprinkle with remaining cheese.

Cheese and Chicken Enchiladas

1 small onion, chopped

1 tablespoon butter

1½ cups cooked shredded chicken breast meat

4 ounces cream cheese

¾ cup shredded cheddar cheese, divided

1 (16 ounce) jar salsa, divided

8 flour tortillas

Sauté onion in butter. Add chicken, cream cheese, ½ cup cheddar, ¾ cup salsa. Heat and stir until cheeses are melted. Spoon ⅓ cup of the mixture into each tortilla. Roll up and place in a lightly greased 9x13-inch baking dish. Spread remaining salsa over tortillas and top with remaining cheese. Cover and bake for 15 to 20 minutes at 350 degrees.

Festive Meat Pie

1 pound ground beef, browned and drained

¼ cup chopped onion

1 (10 ounce) package frozen peas and carrots, thawed

1 cup cooked potatoes, chopped

2 cups cheddar cheese

2 tablespoons flour

½ teaspoon salt

2 tablespoons butter, melted

1 cup water

1 (8 ounce) can refrigerated crescent rolls

Place beef, vegetables, and cheese into baking dish. In a saucepan, add flour and salt to butter; whisk and cook for 2 minutes. Add water and bring to boil, stirring constantly. Simmer on low for 3 minutes. Pour over meat. Unroll dough and place over meat. Press seams together. Bake at 375 degrees for 25 minutes.

Mexican-Style Stuffed Peppers

3 cups cooked white rice
1 cup whole kernel corn
½ cup chopped green onions

1¾ cups salsa, divided
1½ cups cheddar cheese, divided
4 green and 4 red bell peppers,
   halved and seeded

Combine rice, corn, green onions, ¾ cup salsa, and 1 cup cheese in large bowl. Fill each pepper with about ½ cup rice mixture. Place peppers in ungreased 9x13-inch baking dish; top with remaining salsa and cheese. Bake at 350 degrees for 20 to 25 minutes.

Chicken Tacos

1 tablespoon olive oil
1 small sweet onion, chopped
½ teaspoon chili powder
1 (10 ounce) can nacho cheese
    soup

2 (5 ounce) cans chunk chicken,
    drained
8 taco shells
Shredded lettuce
Salsa

Heat oil in skillet. Add onion and chili powder and cook for 1 minute. Add soup and chicken. Heat through, about 4 to 5 minutes. Fill taco shells with mixture. Top with lettuce and salsa.

BBQ Chicken Fajitas

1½ cups instant white rice, uncooked

1½ cups hot water

1 tablespoon taco seasoning mix

4 tablespoons prepared barbecue sauce

4 small boneless, skinless chicken breasts

1 each green and red pepper, cut into strips

½ cup chunky salsa

½ cup Mexican-style finely shredded cheese

Preheat oven to 400 degrees. Combine rice, water, and taco seasoning and spoon onto greased heavy-duty foil or foil packet. Top with remaining ingredients, spreading barbecue sauce on top of the chicken. Seal each packet well, allowing room for the heat to circulate. Bake for 35 minutes or until chicken is no longer pink in the center. Let stand for 5 minutes before serving. Serve with warm tortillas.

As a family, consider eating a simple meal of soup or rice and beans on a weekly basis for one month. Calculate the amount of money you have saved by not serving vegetables and meat and place that amount in a special jar. At the end of the month, donate the money you have saved to a local soup kitchen or to a Christian relief organization such as Samaritan's Purse.

Home-Style Baked Beans

1 (16 ounce) can pork and beans
¼ cup onion
½ teaspoon mustard

¼ cup ketchup
2 tablespoons brown sugar
4 slices bacon, cooked

Combine all ingredients in baking dish; cover and bake at 325 degrees for 1½ hours. Serve with rice, if desired.

Beef and Rice Bowl

3 tablespoons oil

8 ounces frozen oriental vegetables, thawed

8 ounces of deli roast beef, sliced

4 cups cooked rice

¼ teaspoon black pepper

¼ teaspoon soy sauce

¼ teaspoon salt

Heat oil in large fry pan. Add vegetables and beef. Cook 5 minutes stirring constantly. Add rice, pepper, and soy sauce to taste. Cook and stir 5 minutes more. Serve hot.

Crescent Roll Chicken

1 (10 ounce) can cream of chicken soup

½ cup shredded cheddar cheese (optional)

½ cup milk

1 tube refrigerated crescent rolls

3 boneless, skinless chicken breasts, cooked and cut into small pieces

---

Combine soup, cheese, and milk. Pour half in 9x13-inch pan. Separate crescent rolls. Place as much cut-up chicken in each roll as will fit; roll up, tucking in edges. Place in pan. Spoon remaining sauce over rolls. If desired, sprinkle cheese over all. Bake at 350 degrees for 25 to 30 minutes or until lightly browned.

Pepper Steak Stir-Fry

½ cup steak sauce

¼ cup soy sauce

1½ tablespoons cornstarch

1 pound beef top round steak,
   sliced thin

1 tablespoon oil

1 green pepper, cut into strips

1 small sweet onion, sliced

¾ cup beef broth

Mix steak sauce, soy sauce, and cornstarch; coat meat and drain, reserving sauce. Cook and stir meat in hot oil in large skillet for 3 minutes. Add pepper and onion; cook 1 minute. Add beef broth and reserved sauce; bring to boil. Reduce heat; simmer 1 minute. Serve with rice.

Ham Rolls

½ cup margarine
½ tablespoon poppy seeds
½ teaspoon Worcestershire sauce
½ tablespoon mustard
½ tablespoon onion flakes or
  minced onion

1 tube refrigerated biscuits
Baked and sliced ham
Shredded Swiss or mozzarella
  cheese

Melt margarine and stir in poppy seeds, Worcestershire sauce, mustard, and onion; set aside. Top biscuits with ham. Pour margarine mixture over biscuits, sprinkle with cheese, and let set overnight. Bake at 350 degrees for 15 to 20 minutes or until cheese is melted.

Tex-Mex Macaroni Dinner

1 pound lean ground beef
1 red onion, chopped
2 tablespoons taco seasoning
1 cup water
1 (15 ounce) can tomato sauce

8 ounces elbow macaroni, cooked
  and drained
1 (4 ounce) can diced green chilies
1 cup frozen corn
2 cups shredded cheddar cheese

Brown beef and onion. Drain. Add taco seasoning, water, and tomato sauce. Bring to boil and simmer 10 minutes. Stir in cooked macaroni, chilies, and corn. Pour into a greased 13x9-inch baking dish. Top with cheddar cheese. Bake at 350 degrees for 25 minutes.

Festive Winter Chili

1 pound ground beef
1 cup chopped onion
4 minced garlic cloves
1 cup chopped green bell pepper
2 (14 ounce) cans diced tomatoes
1 (8 ounce) can tomato sauce
1½ tablespoons chili powder

1 teaspoon salt
¼ teaspoon cayenne pepper
¼ teaspoon paprika
¼ teaspoon cumin
1 (15½ ounce) can kidney beans
1 tablespoon brown sugar

Brown ground beef with onion, garlic, and bell pepper in large skillet. Drain fat and transfer to a slow cooker. Stir in remaining ingredients and cook on high for 2 hours, stirring occasionally. Refrigerate 24 hours. Reheat in microwave or on stovetop. Serve topped with your favorite chili toppings.

Spaghetti Skilletini

1 (28 ounce) jar pasta sauce
2 cups water
1 (12 ounce) package of spaghetti, broken in half

1 green bell pepper, diced
½ cup shredded mozzarella cheese
½ cup grated Parmesan cheese

In large skillet, combine spaghetti sauce and water. Bring to boil over medium-high heat. Add spaghetti and stir well, making sure spaghetti is completely covered in sauce. Bring to boil again. Cover and reduce heat to low. Simmer for 20 minutes, stirring frequently. Add bell pepper and cook until spaghetti is almost tender. Top with cheeses and serve immediately.

Sometimes the glad tidings of Christmas seem simply too good to be true. But. . . as you keep quiet and listen, you will know deep down in your heart that you are loved. As the air is around about you, so is His love around you. Trust that love. . . . It will never fail.

AMY CARMICHAEL

Family Movie Night
Pizza & Snacks

Lo, children are an heritage of the LORD:
and the fruit of the womb is his reward.

PSALM 127:3

Dad's Famous Pizza Crust

½ cup warm water
1 envelope instant yeast
1¼ cups water, at room temperature
2 tablespoons olive oil
4 cups flour

1½ teaspoons salt
Nonstick cooking spray
Italian seasoning
Garlic powder
Oregano
Basil

In large measuring cup, combine warm water and yeast. Stir immediately. After yeast dissolves (5 minutes or more) stir in room temperature water and oil. Set aside. In large mixing bowl, sift together flour and salt. Begin mixing at low speed as you add the liquid mixture until dough is formed. Knead dough by hand (or in the mixer with the dough hook attachment) until dough is elastic and free of lumps.

Form dough into a ball, and place in bowl greased with cooking spray. Cover tightly with plastic wrap. Let dough rise for 2 hours in a warm area (free from drafts). The dough should double in size.

After dough has doubled, heat oven to 450 degrees as you punch down the dough to deflate. On floured surface, divide dough in half and form 2 smooth dough balls. Cover with slightly damp cloth and allow to rise for no longer than 10 to 15 more minutes.

To bake: Roll out pizza dough and place on pan or pizza stone. Brush both sides of dough with olive oil and sprinkle as desired with Italian seasoning, garlic powder, oregano, and basil. Add your favorite toppings and bake for 12 minutes or until done in center.

Pizza Cups

1 can refrigerated biscuits
Garlic salt
½ cup pizza sauce

1 cup shredded mozzarella cheese
½ teaspoon Italian seasoning
Pizza toppings of your choice

Preheat oven to 375 degrees. Spray 8 regular muffin cups with cooking spray. Sprinkle each cup with a little bit of garlic salt. Divide biscuit dough into 8 equal pieces and press into muffin cups. Sprinkle 1 tablespoon of cheese in the bottom of each muffin cup. Top with a sprinkle of Italian Seasoning and about 1 tablespoon of pizza sauce. Add remaining cheese and top with pizza toppings. Bake for 15 minutes or until done. Allow to cool for a few minutes and then remove from pan. Serve with additional pizza sauce for dipping, if desired.

Hot Vegetable Pizza

1 cup fresh mushrooms, sliced
1 small onion, sliced
1 tablespoon butter

1 large store-bought pizza crust
1 (10 ounce) jar prepared basil pesto
1 large tomato, diced

Sauté mushrooms and onions in butter. Spread crust with pesto. Arrange mushrooms, onion, and tomato on crust. Bake as directed on crust package.

Pizza Bread Sticks

1 (13.8 ounce) tube refrigerated pizza crust
1 tablespoon butter, melted
1 teaspoon garlic salt

¼ teaspoon oregano
1 (8 ounce) jar prepared pizza sauce

Cut pizza crust dough into strips. Place on a greased cookie sheet and brush with butter. Then sprinkle with garlic salt and oregano. Bake at 350 degrees for 12 to 15 minutes or until golden brown. Serve warm with pizza sauce.

Your children are the greatest gift God will give to you, and their souls the heaviest responsibility He will place in your hands. Take time with them, teach them to have faith in God. Be a person in whom they can have faith. When you are old, nothing else you've done will have mattered as much.

LISA WINGATE

Fruit Pizza

1 (20 ounce) package refrigerated sugar cookie dough

1 (8 ounce) package cream cheese, softened

⅓ cup sugar

½ teaspoon vanilla

Assorted fresh fruit, sliced

½ cup raspberry preserves

2 tablespoons cold water

Press cookie dough into a round or rectangle pizza pan. Bake at 375 degrees for 12 minutes or until golden brown. Cool. Meanwhile, beat cream cheese, sugar, and vanilla until smooth. Spread over crust. Arrange fruit over cream cheese layer. Mix preserves and water and spoon over fruit. Refrigerate. Cut into wedges.

BBQ Chicken Pizza

1 large store-bought pizza crust
1 cup barbecue sauce
1 cup cooked chicken, chopped

1 small red onion, sliced
2 cups cheddar cheese

Spread crust with barbecue sauce. Arrange remaining ingredients on crust. Bake as directed on crust package.

English Muffin Pizza

1 English muffin
3 tablespoons spaghetti sauce
¼ cup shredded mozzarella cheese

4 slices pepperoni
Oregano

Split English muffin and place the two halves on baking sheet. Top each muffin half with ½ of the sauce, ½ of the pepperoni, and ½ of the cheese. Sprinkle with a dash of oregano. Bake for 4 to 6 minutes at 350 degrees until cheese is golden brown and bubbly.

Bubble-Up Taco Pizza

2 (16 ounce) tubes refrigerated
  buttermilk biscuits

1½ pounds lean ground beef,
  browned with 1 tablespoon taco
  seasoning

2 cups shredded Cojack cheese

2 cups shredded lettuce

1 small tomato, diced

Salsa

Snip 2 tubes of biscuits into fourths and drop evenly into greased 9x13-inch baking pan. Top with meat mixture and spread evenly over biscuits. Sprinkle cheese over meat. Bake at 350 degrees for about 25 minutes or until biscuits are done in middle. Immediately cover with lettuce and tomato. Drizzle salsa over top and serve.

Snack Kebobs

1 large apple, sliced
5 strawberries, sliced
2 bananas, sliced

Thin pretzel sticks
½ cup orange juice

Dip fruit into orange juice to prevent browning and skewer them onto thin pretzel sticks.

Pinterest is a great place to get ideas for games and family movie nights. There are tons of recipes, theme-night ideas, and wholesome family movie suggestions. Check out my Pinterest board with more great ideas and recipes for family nights at www.pinterest.com/marileeparrish/family-movie-night/

Sweet Snack Mix

1 cup salted roasted peanuts

¼ cup semisweet chocolate chips

1 tablespoon sunflower seeds

¼ cup whole almonds

¼ cup raisins

Combine all ingredients in large bowl. Serve.

Nibble Mix

3 cups mini wheat cereal squares
2 cups popped popcorn
1 cup mini pretzels

¼ cup butter, melted
1 tablespoon Worcestershire sauce
½ teaspoon seasoned salt

Combine cereal, popcorn, and pretzels in microwave-safe bowl. In separate bowl, mix butter, Worcestershire sauce, and salt. Pour over cereal mixture and stir until coated. Microwave for 2 to 3 minutes, stirring after 2 minutes. Stir until well coated. Serve.

Nutty Caramel Corn

12 cups popped popcorn
3 cups almonds
1 cup packed brown sugar
½ cup margarine

¼ cup light corn syrup
½ teaspoon salt
½ teaspoon baking soda

Preheat oven to 200 degrees. Divide popcorn and almonds between two ungreased 9x13-inch baking dishes. Heat brown sugar, margarine, corn syrup, and salt until mixture simmers, stirring constantly. Remove from heat and add baking soda. Pour mixture over popped corn; stir until well coated. Bake for 1 hour, stirring every 15 minutes.

Caramel Popcorn

¼ cup butter

½ cup light corn syrup

1 cup brown sugar

⅔ cup sweetened condensed milk

1 teaspoon vanilla

5 cups popped corn, unpopped hulls removed

Combine butter, corn syrup, and brown sugar. Bring to boil. Stir in condensed milk and return to boil, stirring constantly. Remove from heat and stir in vanilla. Pour over popped corn and stir to coat. With buttered hands, form into balls. Place on waxed paper to set. Makes about 15 popcorn balls.

Uncle Joe's Stovetop Popcorn

½ cup popping corn
1 stick salted butter

Salt, to taste

Add butter to a large pot with a lid. Heat on medium heat until partially melted. Add the popping corn and cover. Move the covered pot back and forth continuously over the heat to evenly distribute and prevent burning. Kernels will begin popping in several minutes. As soon as the popping sounds slow down, remove the pot from the heat. Add salt to taste and serve.

Easy Graham Browns

2 cups crushed graham crackers

1 (14 ounce) can sweetened condensed milk

1 teaspoon vanilla

¾ cup mini semisweet chocolate chips

In medium bowl, blend crushed graham crackers, milk, and vanilla. Stir in chocolate chips. Spread in lightly greased 9x9-inch pan. Bake at 350 degrees for 20 to 25 minutes. Bars may be frosted if desired.

Gail's Mint Chocolate Delights

2 cups flour
⅔ cups baking cocoa
1 teaspoon baking soda
½ teaspoon salt
1 cup butter or margarine

⅔ cup sugar
⅔ cup brown sugar
1 teaspoon vanilla extract
2 eggs
1 (10 ounce) package chocolate and mint morsels

Preheat oven to 325 degrees. Combine flour, cocoa, baking soda, and salt in a small bowl. Beat butter, sugars, and vanilla in a large mixing bowl until creamy. Add eggs, one at a time, beating well after each addition. Gradually beat in flour mixture. Stir in morsels. Drop by tablespoons onto ungreased cookie sheets. Bake for 11 to 13 minutes or until cookies are puffed and centers are set. Cool for 2 minutes before removing from sheets to racks to cool completely.

Chocolate-Drizzled Kettle Corn

2 bags microwave kettle corn

½ cup semisweet or milk chocolate chips

Pop bags of microwave kettle corn and spread in large baking pan. Microwave chocolate chips on high for 30 seconds. Stir. Repeat until chips are melted. Dip a fork into chocolate and drizzle over kettle corn. Allow to cool before serving.

Need-Some-Fiber Cookies!

1 (10 ounce) bag butterscotch chips

1 (10 ounce) bag chocolate chips

1 box fiber cereal (the family-size box that contains 2 bags of cereal)

Melt chips in large bowl in microwave. Mix cereal into melted chips. Drop dollops of mixture onto waxed paper and allow time for them to set. Enjoy!

Chocolate Cookie Brownie Bars

1 (18.3 ounce) box brownie mix

15 chocolate sandwich cookies, crushed

Prepare brownies as directed on box; stir crushed cookies into batter. Pour into greased 9x13-inch pan. Bake as directed on package. Cool and cut into bars.

O star of wonder, star of light,
Star with royal beauty bright,
Westward leading, still proceeding,
Guide us to thy perfect light.

Get-Together Goodies

*When they saw the star, they rejoiced
with exceeding great joy.*

MATTHEW 2:10

Star Cream Cheese Sugar Cookies

1 cup white sugar
1 cup butter, softened (no substitutions)
3 ounces cream cheese, softened
½ teaspoon salt

½ teaspoon vanilla
1 egg yolk
¼ teaspoon baking soda
2¼ cups flour
Powdered sugar

Combine sugar, butter, cream cheese, salt, vanilla, and egg yolk in large mixing bowl. Mix well until smooth. Gradually add baking soda and flour. Blend until cookie dough sticks together. Turn out onto waxed paper and chill for at least 3 hours.

To bake: Roll dough onto surface covered with powdered sugar. Cut into star shapes with a cookie cutter. Bake for 7 minutes at 375 degrees. Ice as desired.

Easy Microwave Fudge

3 cups semisweet chocolate chips   1 teaspoon vanilla

1 (14 ounce) can sweetened
condensed milk

In large microwavable bowl, combine chocolate chips and sweetened condensed milk. Microwave on high for 2 minutes. Add vanilla. Stir. Line 8x8-inch pan with waxed paper and pour in fudge. Refrigerate.

Crunchy Chocolate Cookies

1 cup chow mein noodles
2 cups mini marshmallows
2 cups oats

1 (12 ounce) bag chocolate chips
1 (12 ounce) bag peanut butter
  chips

Combine noodles, marshmallows, and oats in large bowl. Stir. In separate bowl, microwave chocolate and peanut butter chips in 30-second intervals until melted. Pour over noodle mixture and stir to coat. Spoon clumps onto waxed paper and cool.

Leah's Savory Spinach Balls

6 ounces fresh baby spinach

Olive oil

½ medium onion, chopped

1 tablespoon minced garlic

1 (6 ounce) box chicken-flavored stuffing mix

½ cup Parmesan & Romano cheese, grated

3 large eggs

¼ cup melted butter

Wash spinach; drain and pat dry with paper towel. Chop spinach and set aside. In a skillet, add enough olive oil to coat bottom of pan. Over medium heat, add onion and sauté. Then add garlic; sauté for just 30 seconds; then add spinach and, stirring constantly, cook for 2 to 3 minutes. Put into a bowl, add remaining ingredients, and stir until everything is well coated. Using an ice cream scoop or cookie scoop, roll into balls. Bake for 20 minutes at 350 degrees. Serve warm.

Rhonda's Easy Sandwiches

1 can black olives
1 bag raisin bread

1 (8 ounce) block cream cheese

Chop black olives. Mix with cream cheese. Spread on bread. Cut with favorite holiday cookie cutters.

At Christmas, play and make good cheer
For Christmas comes but once a year.

THOMAS TUSSER

Chocolate Pretzel Rings

4 dozen pretzel circles

1 (8 ounce) package milk-chocolate kisses, unwrapped

50 (about ½ cup) candy-coated chocolate pieces

Line cookie sheet with waxed paper. Spread pretzels out on sheet. Place chocolate kiss in center of each pretzel. Bake at 275 degrees for 2 to 3 minutes or until chocolate is softened. Immediately place coated candy on each chocolate kiss and press down slightly so that chocolate spreads to touch pretzel. Refrigerate until chocolate is firm. Store at room temperature.

Sara's Magic Bars

½ cup margarine or butter

1½ cups graham cracker crumbs

1 (14 ounce) can sweetened
condensed milk

1 cup semisweet chocolate chips

1⅓ cups flaked coconut

1 cup chopped nuts

Preheat oven to 350 degrees (or 325 degrees for glass dish). In 9x13-inch baking pan, melt margarine in oven. Sprinkle crumbs over margarine; pour sweetened condensed milk evenly over crumbs. Top with remaining ingredients; press down firmly. Bake 23 to 30 minutes or until lightly browned. Cool. Chill if desired. Cut into bars. Store loosely covered at room temperature.

Leah's Fiesta Party Roll-Ups

2 (8 ounce) packages
cream cheese (softened)
1 (4 ounce) package of fiesta-
style ranch salad dressing
½ cup minced red pepper

½ cup minced celery
¼ cup sliced green onions
¼ cup sliced stuffed olives
3 to 4 (10 inch) soft tortillas

In a mixing bowl, beat cream cheese and dressing mix until smooth. Add red peppers, celery, onions, and olives; mix well. Spread about ¾ cup on each tortilla. Roll up tightly wrap in plastic wrap. Refrigerate for at least 2 hours or overnight. Slice into ½-inch pieces.

Forgotten Mint Kisses

4 egg whites
1 teaspoon cream of tartar
¼ teaspoon salt
1½ cups sugar

1 teaspoon vanilla
Green food coloring
½ package mint chocolate chips

Preheat oven to 350 degrees for 15 minutes. Beat egg whites, cream of tartar, and salt until soft peaks form. Start adding sugar slowly (about 1 tablespoon at a time); continue mixing until all sugar is added and mixture is stiff. Add vanilla and green food coloring. Fold in mint chocolate chips. On greased or parchment paper–lined cookie sheets, drop by small teaspoon size onto sheets. Put in oven; turn off the oven and leave overnight. NO PEEKING! Cookies are done in the morning. Makes 5 dozen cookies.

Rhonda's Sausage Balls

1 pound sausage
10 ounces sharp cheddar cheese
3 cups biscuit baking mix

½ cup milk
2 teaspoons shortening

Brown sausage in skillet and drain. Mix other ingredients in skillet with only 2 teaspoons sausage grease left in it. Roll into balls and bake on greased cookie sheet at 375 degrees until brown.

Once in royal David's city
Stood a lovely cattle shed,
Where a mother laid her baby
In a manger for His bed:
Mary was that mother mild,
Jesus Christ her little child.

CECIL FRANCES ALEXANDER

Fudge Drops

1 cup semisweet chocolate chips, divided

3 tablespoons canola oil

1 cup packed brown sugar

3 egg whites

2 tablespoons plus 1½ teaspoons light corn syrup

1 tablespoon water

2½ teaspoons vanilla extract

1¾ cups flour

⅔ cup plus 1 tablespoon powdered sugar, divided

⅓ cup baking cocoa

2¼ teaspoons baking powder

⅛ teaspoon salt

Preheat oven to 350 degrees. In bowl, combine ¾ cup chocolate chips with oil and melt in microwave; stir until smooth. Pour into large bowl; cool 5 minutes. Stir in brown sugar. Add egg whites, corn syrup, water, and vanilla, and stir until smooth. In separate bowl, combine flour, ⅔ cup powdered sugar, cocoa, baking powder, and salt; gradually add to chocolate mixture until combined. Stir in remaining chocolate chips (dough will be very stiff). Drop by tablespoonfuls 2 inches apart onto greased baking sheets. Bake 10 minutes or until puffed and set. Cool 2 minutes before removing to wire racks. Sprinkle cooled cookies with remaining powdered sugar.

Rhonda's Black Bean Salsa

1 can black beans
1 can shoe peg corn
1 green pepper, chopped
1 purple onion, chopped
4 cups tomato, chopped
¼ cup cilantro, chopped

1 jalapeño, chopped
¼ cup canola oil
Juice of 1 lime
1 teaspoon garlic
1 teaspoon salt

Mix together first 7 ingredients. Combine canola oil, lime, garlic, and salt. Drizzle over top of mixture.

Brownie Pizza

1 (15 ounce) box fudge brownie
    mix, prepared according to
    package directions
½ cup peanut butter

½ cup mini chocolate chips
1 (6 ounce) package candy-coated
    milk-chocolate pieces

Grease 12-inch pizza pan. Pour brownie mix onto pizza pan. Bake at
350 for 15 minutes or until done in center. Remove from oven and let
sit 2 minutes. Drop peanut butter and mini chips onto brownie and let
sit 30 seconds or until peanut butter is melted and easily spreadable.
Spread over brownie and top with candy pieces.

Daddy's Puppy Chow

Melt together: 1 cup chunky peanut butter
1 cup milk-chocolate chips   ½ cup butter

In separate large bowl that has a fitted lid, mix together:

8 cups of Chex cereal   1 cup of peanuts

Add chocolate chip/peanut butter/butter mixture to cereal
mixture. Then add 2 ½ cups powdered sugar. Place lid on bowl and
shake.

Chocolate-Covered Crackers

1½ cups semisweet chocolate chips
1 tablespoon shortening

3 dozen peanut butter sandwich crackers

Combine chocolate chips and shortening in 1-quart saucepan and cook over low heat until melted. Remove from heat; using a fork, dip crackers into mixture until coated. Place on cookie sheet lined with waxed paper and refrigerate until chocolate hardens. If chocolate gets hard while dipping, return saucepan to low heat.

Leah's Reuben Dip

1 (8 ounce) package cream cheese, softened

½ cup sour cream

2 tablespoons ketchup

½ pound deli corned beef, finely chopped

1 cup sauerkraut, chopped, rinsed, and drained

1 cup shredded Swiss cheese

2 tablespoons finely chopped onion

Preheat oven to 350 degrees. In mixing bowl, beat cream cheese, sour cream, and ketchup until smooth. Stir in corned beef, sauerkraut, cheese, and onion. Put in 1-quart baking dish and bake covered for 30 minutes. Uncover and bake 5 minutes more or until bubbly. Serve warm on snack rye bread or crackers. Makes about 3 cups.

Pecan Sugar Balls

½ cup butter
2 tablespoons honey
½ teaspoon vanilla

1 cup flour
2 cups chopped pecans
Red or green sugar sprinkles

Preheat oven to 350 degrees. In small bowl, mix butter and honey with electric mixer. Add vanilla, flour, and pecans; stir well. Shape into 1-inch balls and place on ungreased cookie sheet. Bake for 12 to 14 minutes. Cool slightly and roll in sugar sprinkles.

Love and joy come to you,
And to you your wassail too;
And God bless you and send
you a Happy New Year
And God send you a Happy New Year!

Recipe Index